Introducti

Your body is amazing! It helps you
to walk, work, and play. It helps
you to eat, read, listen, and learn.
It's important to protect your body.

How does your body help you?
How do you protect your body?

Now read and discover
more about your body!

3

Your Skin and Hair

You have skin everywhere on your body. Your skin helps you to touch things. It helps you to know when things are hot or cold. Skin stops dirt getting into your body. It stops water getting into your body when it's rainy and when you swim.

Water on Skin

skin

Hair Standing Up

Sweat on Skin

Hair grows out of your skin. Hair on your arms and legs stands up when you're cold. This stops your body getting too cold. Your skin makes sweat when you're hot. This stops your body getting too hot.

Protect your body! Wash every day, so you can get dirt and sweat off your skin and hair.

Washing

Go to pages 20–21 for activities.

2 Your Bones

There are bones under your skin. These bones make your skeleton. Your skeleton helps you to stand up.

There are joints in your skeleton, too. Bones meet at joints. Elbows and knees are joints. Joints help you to move. Knee joints help you to jump and kick.

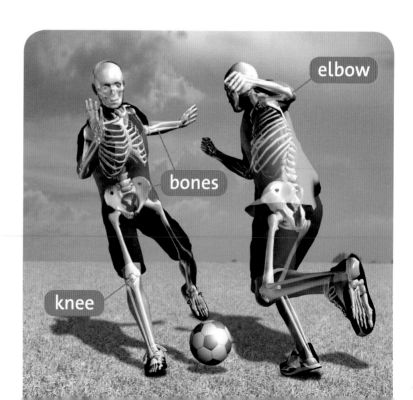

elbow

bones

knee

A baby has small bones. Bones grow and they make you big and tall.

Your bones stop growing when you are about 20 years old. Then there are 206 bones in your body!

Protect your bones! When you ride a skateboard, wear pads to protect your bones and joints. Wear a helmet to protect your head, too.

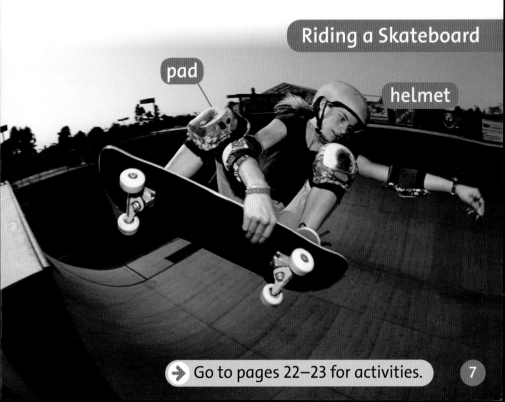

Riding a Skateboard

pad

helmet

Go to pages 22–23 for activities.

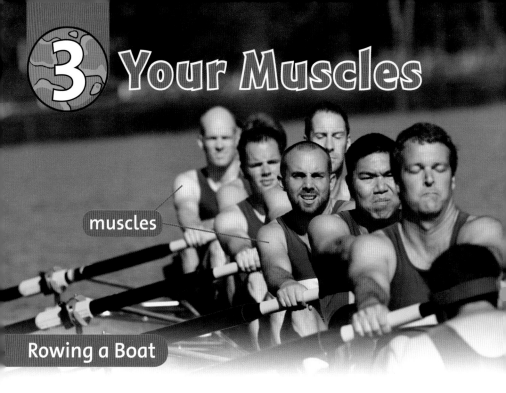

3 Your Muscles

muscles

Rowing a Boat

What helps your bones and joints to walk, run, dance, and jump? Muscles! Muscles pull your bones to move your body. Muscles in your legs help you to ride a bicycle. Muscles in your arms help you to row a boat.

Discover! There are more than 600 muscles in your body!

Running, swimming, dancing, and riding a bicycle are types of exercise. Exercise makes your muscles, bones, and joints strong. Your heart is a type of muscle. Exercise makes your heart strong, too.

Protect your body! Do exercise every day. What is your favorite type of exercise?

Dancing

Go to pages 24–25 for activities.

 # Your Eyes and Ears

Your eyes help you to see the world around you. They open and close many times every day. This is called blinking. When your eyes blink, they wash dirt out of your eyes.

At night your eyes close so you can sleep.

 Eyes blink about 15 times every minute!

Your ears help you to listen to music. They help you to listen for cars in the street. Your ears can hear things when you sleep, too!

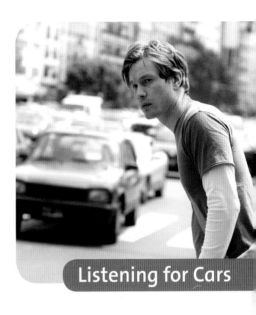
Listening for Cars

Protect your eyes and ears! On sunny days, wear sunglasses to protect your eyes. Don't listen to very loud music – it's bad for your ears.

Protecting Eyes

Go to pages 26–27 for activities.

5 Your Nose and Mouth

You breathe through your nose and mouth. Your nose and mouth take air into your body. You breathe about 15 times every minute.

Breathing Fast

Discover! After exercise, people breathe fast. They can breathe 40 times every minute!

Biting Food

Your nose helps you to smell things. Your mouth helps you to talk and eat. Your teeth bite food so you can eat it. Your body uses food to live and grow.

Protect your teeth! Brush your teeth after breakfast and after dinner, and don't eat lots of candy.

Brushing Teeth

→ Go to pages 28–29 for activities.

6 Your Brain

Do you know how you read these words? Your brain tells you what your eyes see! Your brain tells you what you see, hear, and touch. It tells your muscles when to move. It helps you to write, speak, draw, and do puzzles. Your brain is amazing!

A Brain

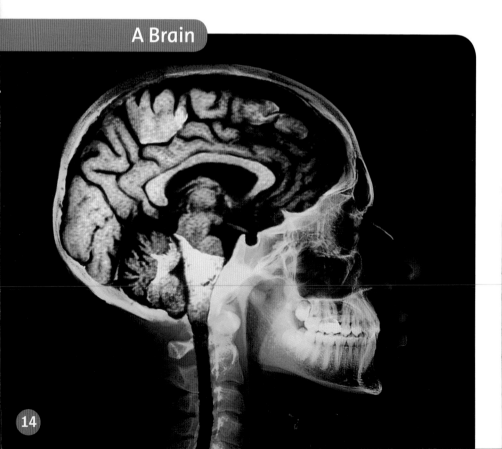

Your brain works all day and at night when you sleep! At night it makes you breathe and it makes your heart work. At night your brain helps you to remember things that you learn in the day.

Protect your brain! Wear a helmet when you ride a bicycle.

helmet

→ Go to pages 30–31 for activities.

7 Getting Sick

Do you get sick? Germs are things that can make you sick. Germs can get in your body when you breathe and when you eat. Germs can get in your mouth from your fingers, too. Some germs get in your body when you get a cut in your skin.

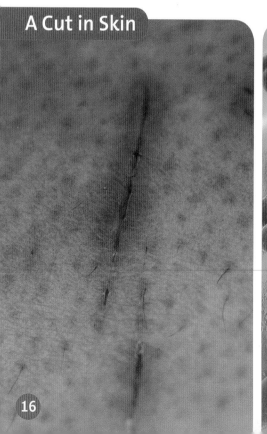

A Cut in Skin

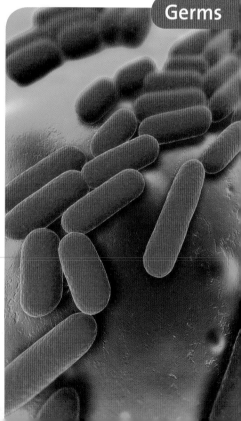

Germs

16

soap

Wash your hands with soap and water to get germs off your fingers. Wash your hands when it's time to eat, after you go to the toilet, after you touch animals, and after you play outside.

Stop germs! There are germs in a sneeze. Catch sneezes in a tissue. Then throw the tissue in a wastebasket.

Catching a Sneeze

tissue

Go to pages 32–33 for activities.

8 Protect Your Body

Eat food that's good for you. Good food helps your bones to grow. It makes you strong, and it stops you getting sick.

Food That's Good for You

There's lots of water in your body. You lose water when you go to the toilet and when your body makes sweat. Drink water every day to protect your body.

Sleeping

Go to the doctor when you get sick, and go to the dentist every year. Do exercise every day. It's good to do exercise and it makes you happy. It's good to sleep when you are tired, too.

It's important to protect your body.

→ Go to pages 34–35 for activities.

1 Your Skin and Hair

← Read pages 4–5.

1 Write the words.   sweat   ~~skin~~   hair   dirt

1 ___skin___   3 _____

2 _____   4 _____

2 Complete the sentences.

dirt   cold   touch   water   ~~body~~

1 You have skin everywhere on your ___body___ .

2 Your skin helps you to _____ things.

3 It helps you to know when things are hot or

_____ .

4 Skin stops _____ getting into your body.

5 It stops _____ getting into your body
when it's rainy.

3 Write *true* or *false*.

1 Hair grows out of your skin.   <u>true</u>

2 Hair on your arms and legs stands
   up when you're hot.   _____

3 Hair stops your body getting
   too cold.   _____

4 Your skin makes sweat when
   you're cold.   _____

5 Sweat stops your body getting
   too hot.   _____

4 Answer the questions.

1 How does your skin help you?
   <u>Your skin helps you to touch things, and</u>
   <u>to know when things are hot or cold.</u>

2 How does your hair help you?

   _____

   _____

3 How can you protect your skin and hair?

   _____

② Your Bones

← Read pages 6–7.

1 Find and write the words.

d	b	b	o	n	e	o	w	s
e	l	b	o	w	b	o	d	y
s	r	j	o	i	n	t	s	o
g	c	k	n	e	e	p	x	t
s	k	e	l	e	t	o	n	e

1 ___bone___

2 _s_____

3 _e_____

4 _k_____

5 _j_____

6 _b_____

2 Circle the correct words.

1 **Muscles / Bones** make your skeleton.

2 Your **skin / skeleton** helps you to stand up.

3 Elbows and knees are **skeletons / joints**.

4 **Bones / Knees** meet at joints.

3 Match. Then write the sentences.

A baby has	in your body.
Bones grow and	when you are about 20 years old.
Your bones stop growing	small bones.
There are 206 bones	they make you big and tall.

1 A baby has small bones.

2 _____

3 _____

4 _____

4 Circle the odd one out.

1 skin (baby) bones

2 joints bones under

3 elbows you knees

4 small bones body

5 joints bones tall

6 pads skateboard wear

3 Your Muscles

← Read pages 8–9.

1 Order the words.

1 bones. / your / Muscles / pull

Muscles pull your bones.

2 help / Muscles / you / a bicycle. / to ride

_____

3 a boat. / Muscles / you / help / to row

_____

4 in / 600 / There / body. / more than / are / your / muscles

_____

2 Find and write the words.

musclesarmslegsbonesjointsbody

1 _muscles_	3 _____	5 _____
2 _____	4 _____	6 _____

3 Write the words.

> running   swimming   jumping   dancing
> walking   riding a bicycle

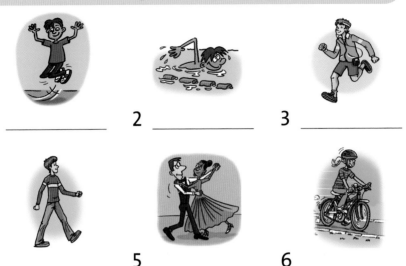

1 _____   2 _____   3 _____

4 _____   5 _____   6 _____

4 Answer the questions.

1 How can you protect your body?

_____

2 Is the heart a type of joint?

_____

3 What makes your heart strong?

_____

4 What is your favorite type of exercise?

_____

4 Your Eyes and Ears

← Read pages 10–11.

1 Match. Then write the sentences.

close many times every day.

Your eyes help you
They open and
When your eyes blink,

to see the world around you.

they wash dirt out of your eyes.

1 _____

2 _____

3 _____

2 Answer the questions.

1 How many times do you blink every minute?

_____

2 How do your eyes help you to sleep?

_____

3 How can you protect your eyes?

_____

3 Circle the correct words.

1 Your ears help you to **see** / **listen to** music.

2 Your ears help you to **listen for** / **move** cars in the street.

3 Your **ears** / **eyes** can hear things when you sleep.

4 Very loud music is **good** / **bad** for your ears.

4 Order the letters and write the words. Then write the secret word.

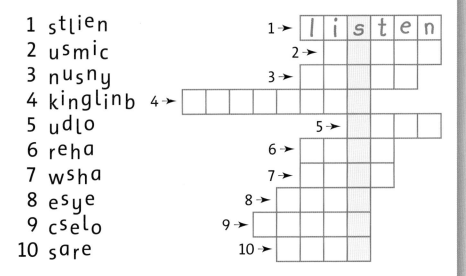

1 stlien

2 usmic

3 nusny

4 kinglinb

5 udlo

6 reha

7 wsha

8 esye

9 cselo

10 sare

1 → l i s t e n

The secret word is:

5 Your Nose and Mouth

← Read pages 12–13.

1 Complete the sentences.

food   nose   breathe

1 Your _____ helps you to smell things.

2 Your teeth bite _____ so you can eat it.

3 You _____ through your nose and mouth.

2 Match. Then write the sentences.

After exercise	air into your body.
Your nose and mouth take	15 times every minute.
People breathe	40 times every minute.
After exercise people can breathe	people breathe fast.

1 _____

2 _____

3 _____

4 _____

3 Write *true* or *false*.

1 Your nose helps you to talk and eat. _____

2 Your teeth smell food. _____

3 Your body uses food to live and grow. _____

4 Brush your teeth to protect them. _____

4 Complete the puzzle.

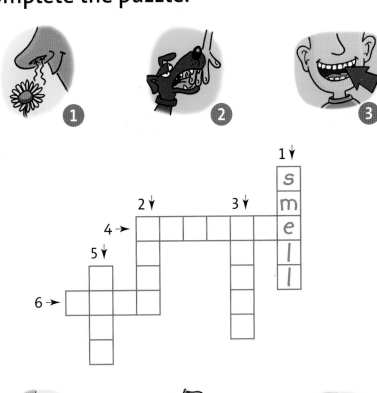

⑥ Your Brain

brain   eyes   hands
muscles   read   speak

1 Write the words.

1 _____

2 _____

3 _____

4 _____

5 _____

6 _____

2 Circle the correct words.

1 Your brain tells you what your eyes
   hear / **see**.

2 Your **brain** / **nose** tells you what you see,
   hear, and touch.

3 Your brain tells your muscles when to
   move / **smell**.

4 Your **brain** / **foot** helps you to write and speak.

3 Order the words.

1 and at night. / Your brain / works all day

_____

2 your brain / you breathe. / At night / makes

_____

3 makes / At night / your heart / your brain / work.

_____

4 remembers things / that you learn. / Your brain

_____

5 a bicycle. / when you ride / Wear a helmet

_____

4 Circle the odd one out.

1 brain   eyes   day
2 bicycle   hand   brain
3 day   night   work
4 hot   brain   heart
5 muscles   learn   read
6 helmet   bicycle   eyes

7 Getting Sick

← Read pages 16–17.

1 Find and write the words.

f	i	n	g	e	r	s	i	r
x	q	b	r	e	a	t	h	e
s	i	c	k	r	q	p	o	l
z	r	u	m	o	u	t	h	x
m	g	e	r	m	s	c	u	t
s	k	i	n	c	s	r	t	w
m	i	n	i	t	o	u	c	h

1 f _____
2 b _____
3 s _____
4 m _____
5 g _____
6 c _____
7 s _____
8 t _____

2 Circle the correct words.

1 Germs are things that can make you
   sick / **happy**.

2 Germs can get in your body when you
   breathe / **touch**.

3 Germs can get in your body when you
   eat / **see**.

4 Germs can get in your mouth on your
   fingers / **toes**.

5 Germs get in your **body** / **bad** when you
   get a cut in your skin.

3 Complete the sentences.

1 Wash hands with _____ and water to get germs off your _____ .

2 It's good to wash your _____ when it's time to _____ and after you go to the toilet.

3 Wash hands after you _____ _____ .

4 There are germs in a _____ .

5 Catch sneezes in a _____ . Then throw the tissue in a _____ .

8 Protect Your Body

← Read pages 18–19.

1 Write the words.

water grow sleep
food protect strong

1 _____

2 _____

3 _____

4 _____

5 _____

6 _____

2 Answer the questions.

1 What food is good for you?

_____

2 How does good food help your bones?

_____

3 What is your favorite food?

_____

3 Match. Then write the sentences.

There's lots of	every day.
You lose water	water when your body makes sweat.
You lose	when you go to the toilet.
Drink water	water in your body.

1 _____

2 _____

3 _____

4 _____

4 Complete the sentences.

doctor   water   dentist
exercise   sleep   food

1 Eat _____ that's good for you.

2 Drink _____ every day.

3 Go to the _____ when you get sick.

4 Go to the _____ every year.

5 Do _____ every day.

6 It's good to _____ when you are tired.

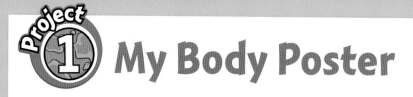
My Body Poster

1 Choose a part of the body. Write notes and complete the diagram.

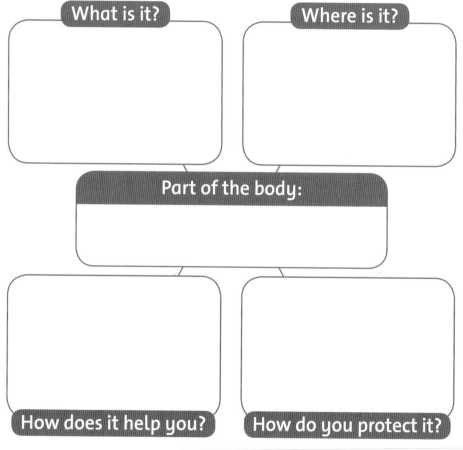

What is it?

Where is it?

Part of the body:

How does it help you?

How do you protect it?

2 Find or draw pictures of the part of the body. Make a poster.

3 Display your poster.

An Exercise Graph

1 **Ask four friends what exercise they do. Complete the chart.**

Do you ...	Friend 1	Friend 2	Friend 3	Friend 4
swim?				
dance?				
run?				
walk?				
ride a bicycle?				
ride a skateboard?				

2 **Draw a graph.**

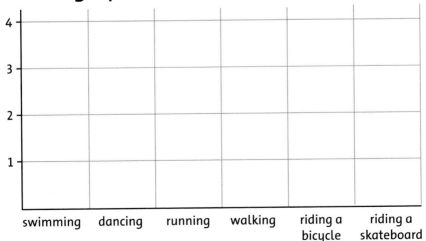

Picture Dictionary

 around

 bite

 blink

 body

 bone

 brain

 breathe

 cut

 dirt

 exercise

 fast

 food

 grow

 hair

 joints

 lose

loud

 minute

 muscles

 protect

 pull

 remember

 skeleton

 skin

 smell

 sneeze

 soap

 street

 strong

 sunglasses

 sweat

 world

Oxford Read and Discover

Series Editor: Hazel Geatches • CLIL Adviser: John Clegg

Oxford Read and Discover graded readers are at six levels, for students from age 6 and older. They cover many topics within three subject areas, and support English across the curriculum, or Content and Language Integrated Learning (CLIL).

Available for each reader:
• Audio CD Pack (book & audio CD)
• Activity Book

Teaching notes & CLIL guidance: www.oup.com/elt/teacher/readanddiscover

Subject Area / Level	The World of Science & Technology	The Natural World	The World of Arts & Social Studies
1 300 headwords	• Eyes • Fruit • Trees • Wheels	• At the Beach • In the Sky • Wild Cats • Young Animals	• Art • Schools
2 450 headwords	• Electricity • Plastic • Sunny and Rainy • Your Body	• Camouflage • Earth • Farms • In the Mountains	• Cities • Jobs
3 600 headwords	• How We Make Products • Sound and Music • Super Structures • Your Five Senses	• Amazing Minibeasts • Animals in the Air • Life in Rainforests • Wonderful Water	• Festivals Around the World • Free Time Around the World
4 750 headwords	• All About Plants • How to Stay Healthy • Machines Then and Now • Why We Recycle	• All About Desert Life • All About Ocean Life • Animals at Night • Incredible Earth	• Animals in Art • Wonders of the Past
5 900 headwords	• Materials to Products • Medicine Then and Now • Transportation Then and Now • Wild Weather	• All About Islands • Animal Life Cycles • Exploring Our World • Great Migrations	• Homes Around the World • Our World in Art
6 1,050 headwords	• Cells and Microbes • Clothes Then and Now • Incredible Energy • Your Amazing Body	• All About Space • Caring for Our Planet • Earth Then and Now • Wonderful Ecosystems	• Food Around the World • Helping Around the World